ANIMAL RELATIVES

DOGS and WOLVES

CANINE RELATIVES

by Heather E. Schwartz

PEBBLE
a capstone imprint

Published by Pebble, an imprint of Capstone
1710 Roe Crest Drive, North Mankato, Minnesota 56003
capstonepub.com

Library of Congress Cataloging-in-Publication Data
is available on the Library of Congress website.

ISBN: 9798875220326 (hardcover)
ISBN: 9798875220272 (paperback)
ISBN: 9798875220289 (ebook PDF)

Summary: Dogs and wolves sometimes look alike. Can they possibly be related? Explore the many amazing ways dogs and wolves are alike and different. Learn all about the habitats, skills, life cycles, and features of these canine relatives.

Editorial Credits
Editor: Ashley Kuehl; Designer: Bobbie Nuytten; Media Researcher: Svetlana Zhurkin; Production Specialist: Whitney Schaefer

Image Credits
Getty Images: 500px/Bill Boss, 24, Andyworks, 28, Jupiterimages, 7, nigelb10, 17, YakobchukOlena, 19; Shutterstock: arthurgphotography, 12, Debbie Steinhausser, 15, Geoffrey Kuchera, 22, Holly Kuchera, 21, Katho Menden, 27, KensCanning, 20, Lenti Hill, 25, Maria Moroz, 9, Mary Swift, 4, Masarik, cover (top), matushaban, 18, Prostock-studio, 16, Pupsiki, 29, riansa28 (background), cover, 1, 30, Rudmer Zwerver, cover (bottom), 5, scigelova, 13, Sharon Feragotti, 23, sirtravelalot, 11, Wirestock Creators, 6, 14

Printed and bound in China. PO 006276

TABLE OF CONTENTS

Words in **bold** are in the glossary.

DOG OR WOLF?

That animal has four legs and a tail. Is it a dog? Is it a wolf? Can you tell the difference? It's not always easy. Many look almost exactly alike.

Wolves and dogs are related. Wolves were around first. Dogs **evolved** from wolves. It took thousands of years. Dogs became **domestic** animals. Wolves remain wild. How else are dogs and wolves alike and different? Let's find out!

FIRST CLUE: PHYSICAL FEATURES

Wolf and dog bodies are different. A wolf's skull is larger than a dog's skull. Its jaw is bigger and stronger. Wolves' feet are also much larger than dogs' feet. Wolves have long middle toes on their front feet. This helps them run fast and far.

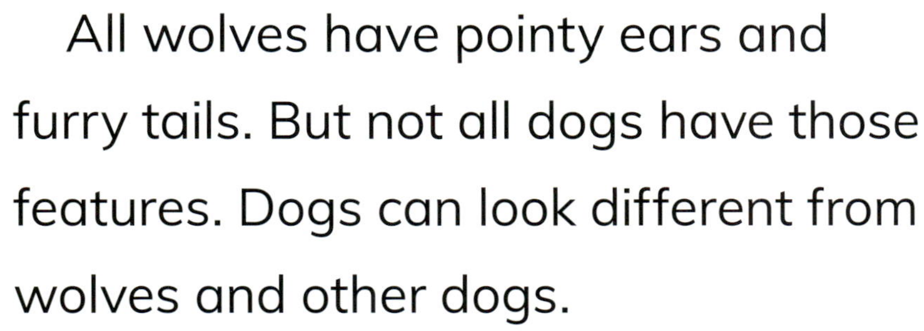

All wolves have pointy ears and furry tails. But not all dogs have those features. Dogs can look different from wolves and other dogs.

As dogs evolved, different **breeds** did too. Some have pointy ears and long **snouts**. They have gray, white, and tan coloring. But others don't look like wolves at all. Basset hounds have short legs and floppy ears. Dachshunds have long, low bodies. They have reddish-brown coats. And pugs have short snouts. They have curly tails.

FUN FACT

Pugs look a bit like pigs. But they're not related!

Huskies look a lot like wolves. But they are dogs.

SENSES SET THEM APART

Dogs and wolves experience the world differently than humans do. Their senses are stronger. Dogs' noses sniff more than dinner. They use their sense of smell for many jobs. They identify other dogs and certain people. They smell people's sweat. That tells them when people are afraid. They can hear sounds humans can't.

FUN FACT

Dogs can smell 1,000 to 10,000 times better than humans!

CAUTION
CAUTION
CAUTION

Wolves have even better senses than dogs. Wolves can hear sounds up to 6 miles (9.7 kilometers) away. They can smell scents almost 2 miles (3.2 km) away. These senses help them hunt **prey**. They can defend themselves from **predators**.

HOME SWEET HOME

Home means different things to different creatures. This is true for wolves and dogs too. Wolves live in packs with other wolves. They roam forests and grasslands. They travel mountains and deserts.

Wolves sleep in grass, under trees, and in bushes. Before a wolf has babies, she digs a den. She picks a safe place to care for them.

Most dogs don't live in packs. They live with people. But they do form social groups with their human friends. Some experts call this a pack. Others say these groups are different from packs.

Dogs live everywhere people do. They live on farms, in cities, and in the suburbs.

Human homes and fences keep them safe. Predators and bad weather don't usually harm them.

DINNERTIME!

Have you ever called a dog to dinner? They come running! Most dogs can run 15 to 20 miles (24 to 32 km) per hour.

Dogs need humans to feed them. They can eat some people foods. Carrots and blueberries are safe. But they mostly eat dog food made of fish, chicken, or beef. Raw meat is off limits to pet dogs. It can make them sick.

Wolves run at dinnertime too. But that's because they have to hunt! Their average speed is 36 to 38 miles (58 to 61 km) per hour. That's much faster than dogs. This helps them catch their prey.

Nobody serves meals to wild wolves. So they eat when they can. They sometimes eat a lot. Then they go for days or weeks without food. Most of what they eat is raw meat.

FUN FACT

A wolf can eat as much as 20 pounds (9 kilograms) of food at a time!

PLAYING AND PROBLEM-SOLVING

Everyone loves to play, right? Wolves and dogs sure do. Wolf pups pounce, stalk, and learn to hunt. Dogs don't need those skills. But play teaches puppies how their bodies work.

FUN FACT

Scientists have found that some wolf pups can learn to play fetch!

Adult wolves play with other wolves. Dogs play with other dogs and with humans. Running, chasing, and rolling around are fun for all **canines**!

Wolves are good at solving problems. They may see something good to eat. It might be hard to reach. But they can figure out how to get it. They don't need help from humans.

Dogs do need help. Humans give them food. Dogs can be trained, though. They can learn to solve problems. They can learn to get their own treats.

CANINE COMMUNICATION

Wolves use scent, sound, and body language to talk. Dogs do too! Both animals mark their **territory**. They leave the odor of their urine. They bark and howl to warn of danger. They show anger with bared teeth. They show fear with ears flat against their heads. When they feel friendly, they dance around. They seem to ask, "Want to play?"

But there is one big difference between wolves and dogs. Wolves talk with other wolves and wild animals.

FUN FACT

Dogs and wolves can understand each other's signals and body language!

Dogs spend time with people. So they talk to humans too. Dogs have a small muscle above their eyes. It helps them show their feelings. They make humanlike faces! That lets them connect with people.

CAN YOU REMEMBER?

1. What is one dog breed that looks like a wolf?

2. Are pugs related to pigs or wolves?

3. Which animal runs faster, a dog or a wolf?

4. Why do wolf pups play?

5. Which animal makes humanlike faces, a dog or a wolf?

Check your answers at the bottom of page 31!

ANIMAL JOKES

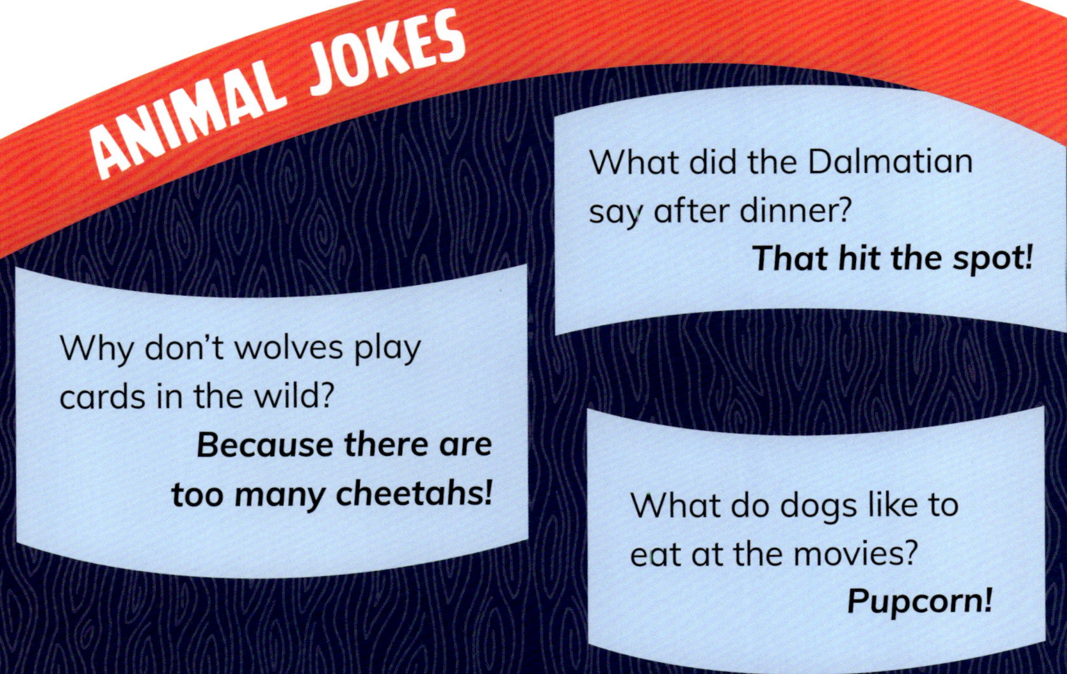

What did the Dalmatian say after dinner?

That hit the spot!

Why don't wolves play cards in the wild?

Because there are too many cheetahs!

What do dogs like to eat at the movies?

Pupcorn!

GLOSSARY

breed (BREED)—a certain type of animal within a species

canine (KAY-nine)—an animal that is part of the dog family

domestic (duh-MES-tik)—lives with humans

evolve (ih-VAHLV)—to develop over time

predator (PRED-uh-tur)—an animal that hunts others

prey (PRAY)—an animal that is hunted for food

snout (SNOUT)—the nose and mouth of an animal

territory (TER-i-tor-ee)—an area that an animal claims for itself

1. A husky; 2. Wolves; 3. A wolf; 4. To learn to hunt and because it's fun; 5. A dog

INDEX

ABOUT THE AUTHOR

Heather E. Schwartz is an award-winning children's book author in upstate New York. She lives with her husband, two kids, and two cats named Stampy and Squid. As a child, she had a mixed-breed dog she loved named Muffin.